Cows
Have No
Top Teeth

Kelly Tills

Copyright © 2021 Kelly Tills
Paperback Edition

ISBN: 978-1-955758-69-7

A division of FDI publishing LLC

The lovely thing
about cows is...

cows have no
top teeth!

Kids lose their top teeth, but they grow back. Snails have teeth on their tongues.

Narwhals have a head tooth!

Does a cow need a straw to eat grass?

No!
They are super good chewers.

Does a cow whistle a
happy tune?

No!
But they love music.

Does a cow smile?

Yes,
they have lovely
smiles.

Cows have a hard spot in their mouth instead of top teeth.

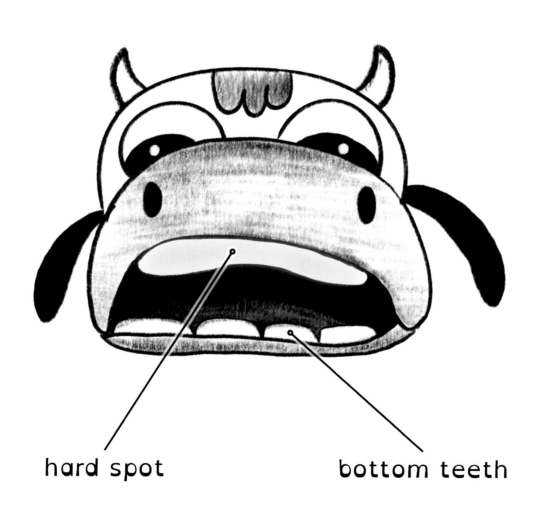

hard spot

bottom teeth

They bite grass between their bottom teeth and the hard spot to get it out of the ground.

yummy grass

When a cow eats, it's called

grazing.

Does a cow graze all day?

Yes, they chomp and chew until they're full.

Does a cow graze all night?

No, they sleep.
(But I bet they dream about chewing!)

When cows graze, they save their food for later by swallowing it.

When they finish, they get comfy and spit it all back up.

And they chew it all over again!

Cows really love chewing.

And that's the lovely
thing about cows.

What's the lovely thing about **you?**

Well, actually...

one type of bull (which is a male cow) *did* learn how to whistle. They do it to warn others of danger.

Whoa! That's crazy.

Get More *Awesome Animals* Books

About the Author

Kelly Tills writes silly books for kids and believes even the smallest hat-tip, in the simplest books, can teach our kids how to approach the world. Kelly's children's stories are perfect to read aloud to young children, or to let older kids read themselves (hey, let them flex those new reading skills!). Proud member of the *International Dyslexia Association*.

I hope this book brought you and your tiny human some fun time together. Help others find this book, and experience that same joy by **leaving a review!**

Point your phone's camera here.

It'll take you straight to the review page. Magic!

Made in the USA
Monee, IL
19 April 2023